The Truth about

ISHMAEL

JGB

The Truth about Ishmael

ISBN 979-8-9897556-6-0

Cover designed using ChatGPT.

For millennia Muslims have claimed they are an Abrahamic faith through Ishmael, Abraham's first son, and therefore are not only descendants of Abraham, but are the only legitimate and superior ones among the Jews and Christians who also claim the same inheritance. However, what is the truth?

The only true historical record among sacred script about Abraham or Ishmael is in the Bible—the Hebrew Bible to be exact, in the Book of Genesis. This sacred book was written by Moses around 1440-1400 BC and details the birth of Abraham (nee Abram) and his two sons, Ishmael and Isaac (Genesis 12-27). No historical record of Ishmael or his descendants appeared outside biblical sources until vague inscriptions in Assyrian and Babylonian culture in the 9th and 8th centuries BC, 500-600 years later.[i] Muslims cannot produce any historical records of their own detailing the lives or existence of Abraham or Ishmael.

For centuries Muslim scholars and clerics have trumpeted that the Bible is corrupt and unreliable. Yet, they must rely on it for the story of Ishmael because they have no authentic or reliable source of their own on who Ishmael was and how he fits into their history.

What does the Qur'an say about Ishmael? Ishmael (i.e. Ismail in the Qur'an) appears 12 times by name in the Qur'an, but only once by himself. All other references to Ismail in the Qur'an are in association with biblical persons, notably Abraham (Ibrahim), Isaac (Ishaq) and Jacob (Yaqoub) five times.[ii] The Bible provides 54 references in the Old Testament that link directly to Ishmael.

Although Ismail holds a key role in the Islamic narrative, the Qur'an is mostly silent of Ismail's relationship to Ibrahim (Abraham) or Allah's plan for him. The Bible, however, provides details which will be presented later. The Qur'an does offer some interesting verses of Ismail's connection with biblical persons (also to be presented later).

3

According to Muslim "tradition" and not historical fact, Muhammad and Arabic Muslims are descendants of Ishmael. However, they cannot produce any such genealogical, historical or archeological evidence outside Islamic sources as proof of their assertions. Yet, Muslims firmly believe that Ishmael (*Ismail* in the Qur'an) was a prophet and ancestor of Muhammad and that Ishmael was the first Muslim to speak Arabic fluently. Outside Islam there is no such verification.

Muslims also claim that even Adam, the first man of creation, spoke Arabic. So, what is the truth? According to non-Muslim historic sources, Arabic was not a spoken language until the 8th century BC, or 13 centuries after the birth of Ishmael.[iii] As far as Ishmael's genealogy, the Qur'an is silent. It does not mention the 12 sons of Ishmael, only the Bible does (Genesis 25:12-18; 1 Chronicles 1:28-31).

Even the Islamic website, *Alif Arabic*, states: "The earliest known form of the Arabic language is Old Arabic, which was spoken in the 4th century CE" or 17 centuries after the birth of Ishmael.[iv] The same source later states that: "No one knows exactly when the Arabic language started. Historically the oldest written Arabic manuscript was from the fourth-century CE. Some linguists estimate the date to be about 1600 or 1000 years ago." Clearly, Ishmael/Ismail could not have spoken a language that did not exist.

Another reference to Ismail in the Qur'an is in surah 14:39 which claims that Allah granted Ismail and Ishaq (Isaac) *old age*. There is no further clarification. Likely because whoever wrote this section of the Qur'an (and yes, there were likely numerous authors) did not know. However, if they had read the Bible they would have known. The Bible clearly states that Ishmael lived to be 137 years old (Genesis 25:17) and Isaac was the longest living patriarch at 180 (Genesis 35:28).

One of Islam's Greatest Deceptions & Fabrications. One of the greatest deceptions in Islam is the perversion of Ishmael's biblical role as stated in Surah 37:102-105. Who did God ask Abram/Abraham to sacrifice: Ishmael or Isaac? To fully understand the context of the remainder of this section, one must understand that the god of the Muslims, Allah, is not the God of the Bible.

Whoever therefore turns back after this [Allah's covenant through the prophets (of the Bible) and subsequent revelation of Muhammad (not by name) as a prophet in surah 3:81], *these it is that are the transgressors* (surah 3:82). So, anyone who violates Allah's covenant that he made through the prophets, and by extension, Muhammad, is opposed to Allah.

Now, here is the first point. Prior to Muhammad—despite Islam's appropriation of biblical prophets—there were NO Muslim prophets. So, who were the "prophets" referred to in surah 3:81?

Say: We believe in Allah and what has been revealed to us, and what was revealed to Ibrahim [Abraham] *and Ismail* [Ishmael] *and Ishaq* [Isaac] *and Yaqoub* [Jacob] *and the tribes, and what was given to Musa* [Moses] *and Isa* [Jesus] *and to the prophets from their Lord; we do not make any distinction between any of them, and to Him do we submit* (surah 3:84). Interesting!

Allah, it should be noted, did not reveal anything through the prophets of the Bible, or through the prophets of the Hebrews or Christians. This is all Islamic slight-of-hand, that is, biblical theft, to create a narrative that Islam did not and does not have. If Muslims truly believe that Allah revealed his truths through the prophets of the Bible, then they must accept the Bible as unadulterated truth. However, they do not.

In Islam's version of God's call to Abraham to sacrifice his son as a test of faith, the Qur'an never mentions the name of Abraham's son. However, Muslims since the inception of Islamic ideology have vehemently claimed that it was Ismail that Ibrahim was called to sacrifice.

And when he [Ismail] *attained to working with him* [Ibrahim], *he said: O my son! Surely I have seen in a dream that I should sacrifice you; consider then what you see. He said: O my father! Do what you are commanded; if Allah please, you will find me of the patient ones.*

So when they both submitted and he threw him down upon his forehead, and We^v called out to him saying: O Ibrahim!

You have indeed shown the truth of the vision; surely thus do We reward the doers of good;

Notice that the Qur'an and Muslims attribute Abraham (Ibrahim) as the father of Ishmael. Whereas the Bible clearly states that *Abram* was the father of Ishmael. Yes. it is the same man, but there is a significant spiritual difference which will be addressed later.

Another interesting verse in the Qur'an is surah 4:163 (note, the use of [ ] is a later insertion into the verse by an Islamic scribe in some versions of the Qur'an).

Surely We have revealed to you [O Muhammad] *as We revealed to Nuh* [Noah], *and the prophets after him, and We revealed to Ibrahim and Ismail and Ishaq* [Isaac] *and Yaqoub* [Jacob] *and the tribes, and Isa* [Jesus] *and Ayub* [Job] *and Yunus* [Jonah] *and Haroun* [Aaron] *and Sulaiman* [Solomon] *and We gave to Dawood* [David] *Psalms.*

To take a more investigative look at this Qur'anic verse, who were the prophets after Noah? First, Noah was a pivotal figure in the Bible narrative of God's judgment on wickedness, not the Qur'an or in Islamic history. The prophets that *followed after him* included Abraham, Isaac, Jacob, Aaron (Moses' brother), Moses, Samuel, Elijah, Elisha, Isaiah, Jeremiah, Ezeliel, Daniel and many others in the Bible. None of them were Muslim prophets as the scribes of Islam claim and none of them prophesied a word about the coming of Muhammad. Many of them did, however, prophesy over 300 times about the coming of God's one and only Son who would bring salvation to all of mankind if they would accept His Gospel message of deliverance from sin, that is the one and only Prince of Peace, Jesus Christ.

Abraham's Ancestry. To understand this conflicting relationship and view of Abram/Abraham, it is necessary to recognize Abram's true ancestry as revealed in Genesis, chapter 11. Abram's journey with the God of the Bible started in Ur of the Chaldeans in Mesopotamia.

Now the LORD had said to Abram: "Get out of your country, from your family and from your father's house, to a land that I will show you. I will make you a great nation; I will bless you and make your name great; and you shall be a blessing. I will bless those who bless you, and I will curse him who curses you; and in you all the families of the earth shall be blessed" (Genesis 12:1-3).

Where was Ur? It would be in current-day Iraq, northwest of the Persian Gulf. Now, here is the interesting part. The Chaldeans were not Arab, they were a Semitic people with their own unique ethnicity, language and culture that predated the arrival of Arabs.[vi] There is no historical evidence that a people known as Arabs (i.e. nomads) existed before the ninth century BC.
In addition, the language the Chaldeans spoke was Aramaic (the tongue spoken by Jesus) and not Arabic (it did not exist at that time). Today, most Chaldeans are Christian and do not trace any ancestry to Arabs, Muslims or the Islamic ideology.

It is notable that the Qur'an is silent on Abraham's ancestry and on his call from God to leave Ur and travel to a non-Arab nation. Odd that this very important piece of the Islamic story is left out.

Why? Because it does not exist and has no place in the Muslim narrative.

Abram's father was Terah (Genesis 11:26) who was a direct descendant of Noah. It is estimated that Abram was born about 2166 B.C., or about 12-13 centuries <u>before</u> the arrival of the Arab peoples.

What does the Bible say about Ishmael? It is in Genesis 16 of the Bible that the story of Ishmael first unfolds. The name of Ishma<u>el</u> is Hebrew and not Arabic. It means, "God (el) hears" (Genesis 16:11). Abram (Hebrew for "High Father") was Ishmael's father. Abraham (Hebrew for "Father of a Multitude") was Isaac's father. The distinction is critical as you will soon see.

Ishmael was not an Arab. He was not even half Arab. His father, as noted previously, was of the Chaldeans. His mother, the Egyptian Hagar, was Sarai's (i.e. Sarah's) handmaid and became Abram's concubine and the mother of Ishmael. So, Ishmael was half Chaldean and half Egyptian, neither lineage was Arab.

Notice too, that Ishmael was given a Hebrew name. He was not born with the moniker of Muhammad, Mohamed, Abdul, Abdullah, Ahmed, Ali, Omar or any other popular Arabic names.

Egyptians are not genealogically nor genetically linked to Arabs, nor are they descendants of Ishmael. Impossible! Egyptians only became "Arabs" in name only after they were violently conquered by murderous Muslim hordes in 639-642 A.D. Prior to the Muslim conquest most of the Egyptian population was Christian.

So, what does the Bible say about the controversial figure of Ishmael? His character? God's covenant? His descendants? Future prophecy? While the Qur'an is mostly silent on these issues, the Bible provides great detail and insight.

8

What about Egypt, the place of Ishmael's birth? Egypt is only mentioned 5 times in the Qur'an, of which all five are in reference to biblical stories that are not of Qur'anic origin. In contrast, Egypt is mentioned 660 times in the Bible since it plays a key role in the biblical narrative.

An estimated 2,500 years before the supposed arrival of Muhammad, the God of the Bible promised the Land of Canaan to Abraham and his descendants (c.1918 BC). Interestingly, the Qur'an confirms this promise in surah 5:20-21.

In the Land of Canaan, God spoke to Abram and made this covenant with him:

But Abram said, "Lord GOD, what will You give me, seeing I go childless, and the heir of my house is Eliezer of Damascus?" Then Abram said, "Look, You have given me no offspring; indeed one born in my house is my heir!"

And behold, the word of the LORD came to him, saying, "This one [Eliezer] shall not be your heir, but one who will come from your own body shall be your heir." Then He brought him outside and said, "Look now toward heaven, and count the stars if you are able to number them." And He said to him, "So shall your descendants be."

And he believed in the LORD, and He accounted it to him for righteousness (Genesis 15:2-6).

When Abram was in his mid-80s, he was still without a true heir from Sarai's womb. So, Sarai took matters into her own hands and gave Abram Hagar to fulfill God's promise of an heir (Genesis 16:1-4). This was not God's plan, nor promise, but the will of Abram and Sarai's flesh to bring about what God had promised. Muslim "tradition" claims Hagar was Abraham's wife and not his concubine and Sarai's handmaid.

Ishmael was born when Abram was 86 years old. Before Ishmael's birth, an angel appeared to Hagar with this prophecy about her son:

And the Angel of the LORD said to her: "Behold, you are with child, and you shall bear a son. You shall call his name Ishmael, because the LORD has heard your affliction. He shall be a wild man; his hand shall be against every man, and every man's hand against him. And he shall dwell in the presence of all his brethren" (Genesis 16:11-12).

Once again, Muslims "claim" that Ishmael was a righteous apostle/prophet. However, the Bible verses above clearly state otherwise.

Who are or were the Ishmaelites? Although certain non-Muslim sources tend to support the "theory" that some Arabs, not all, may be able to trace their heritage to Ishmael, other sources claim it is genetically impossible to do so. If Muslim Arabs want to cling to the myth that they are descendants of Ishmael, then this is God's promise to them in Genesis 16:11-12).

The Bible does mention the descendants of Ishmael, the Ishmaelites, several times, but the Qur'an never mentions them. Genesis 37:25-28 mentions that Joesph's jealous brothers sold him to Ishmaelite traders from Gilead, a region just east of the Jordan River and south of the Sea of Galilea—an area on western most border of current-day Jordan, near the border of Israel.

Judges 7 & 8 of the Bible is the story of Gideon who was called of God to go against the army of the Midianites and Amalekites and "all the sons of the east were lying in the valley as numerous as locusts; and their camels were without number, as numerous as the sand on the seashore" (Judges 7:12). The Midianites were Ishmaelites and God told Gideon to take them on with only 300 men (Judges 7:7-8). After Gideon's complete victory, the Bible states that the Ishmaelites had crescent ornaments around their camel's necks and wore gold earrings (Judges 8:21 and 24).

As important as Ishmael is to the Muslim narrative, the Qur'an is once again silent on his ancestry. The Bible, however, names Ishmael's 12 sons and where they settled (Genesis 25:12-18).

Ishmael's sons, as listed in Genesis 25, were:
Nebaioth, meaning "fruitfulness"
Kedar, meaning "dark" or "swarthy"
Adbeel, or "God's discipline"
Mibsam, "fragrant aroma"
Mishma, "rumor" or "report"
Dumah, "silence" or "death"
Massa, "burden" or "oracle"
Hadad, "thunder" or "noise"
Tema, "south country"
Jetur, "enclosure" or "encampment"
Naphish, "he that rests"
Kedemah, "eastward" or "Oriental"

Note that the sons of Ishmael had Hebrew names and were born long before Arabic was created as a language.

Ishmael's descendants, the Ishmaelites, are known to have settled in a territorial band from Egypt, the Wilderness of Paran, the northern Arabian desert and in the Land of Canaan (Genesis 25:18). They were not Arabs, nor did they speak Arabic, as Muslims claim, but the Semitic language of the Canaanites.

Ishmaelites, it appears, may have ceased to exist as a people or had been absorbed into other cultures as early as the 10th century BC or over 1500 years before the Muslim-attributed birth of Muhammad.[vii]

The evidence indicates that Ishmael was not the father of the Arabs, and neither was Abraham. The Ishmaelites were probably

Canaanites, speaking, not an early form of Arabic, but a dialect similar to Hebrew. In time they disappeared or were absorbed into other groups, like so many other ancient peoples.[viii]

God's Covenant was with Abraham and Isaac, not with Abram and Ishmael. Although Muslims insist that it was Ishmael that Allah called Abraham to sacrifice, the Qur'an curiously does not mention the name of Abraham's son to be offered to Allah (recall surah 37:102-107, cited previously). The only source of this Islamic fabrication is Muslim "tradition" and not historical nor biblical fact.

To some, including many Christian leaders, the preceding title may be judged as insignificant or trivial. However, it is very important to address and understand. While many biblical scholars and teachers make no distinction between Abram and Abraham, there is a clear spiritual separation. The God of the Bible made three promises to Abram/Abraham under three different circumstances. The God of the Bible did not make a covenant with Abram and Ishmael to fulfill His covenant with Abraham.

To link Islam with the seed of Abraham was an attempt by early Islamic leaders to gain favor with Jewish and Christian communities. In an effort to usurp the Abrahamic lineage for Islam, Muslim clerics and scholars have proclaimed for centuries that it was not Isaac—the Jewish patriarch that spawned the 12 tribes of Israel and that Abraham sought to sacrifice on Mount Moriah in Jerusalem—but rather it was Ishmael that God called Abraham to sacrifice on Mount Mina outside Mecca in Saudi Arabia.

Promise #1. In Genesis 12:1-2, God promised *Abram* that he would be the head of a great nation and that whoever blessed Abram, God would bless.

Now the LORD had said to Abram: "Get out of your country, from your family and from your father's house, to a land that I will show you. I will make you a great nation; I will bless you and make your name great; and you shall be a blessing. I will bless those who bless you, and I will curse him who curses you; and in you all the families of the earth shall be blessed."

Prior to God's calling, Abram was a Chaldean pagan from Ur. God Almighty saw something in Abram that set him apart from his countrymen, so God called him to leave Ur with his family and made him the preceding promise. As a result of Abram's faithfulness, he became the first Hebrew Patriarch.[ix]

Promise #2. Remember in Genesis 15 God promised Abram that he would have a son of his own flesh, i.e., a son from Sarai's own womb. Years passed and Abram was now 86 years old and still without a son, so he and Sarai decided to help God fulfill His promise. Sarai offered her handmaid, Hagar, to conceive Abram's son (Genesis 16:3-4). Sarai became jealous of Hagar's pregnancy and birth of a son and treated Hagar with contempt. Hagar the Egyptian fled into the wilderness of Shur (Genesis 16:7). At the end of Genesis 16, it is Abram that names his son Ishmael (God hears). This is significant as you will see.

Promise #3. When Ishmael was 13 years old and his father, Abram was 99, the LORD spoke to Abram and said:

"I am Almighty God [El Shaddai]*; walk before Me and be blameless. And I will make My covenant between Me and you, and will multiply you exceedingly." Then Abram fell on his face, and God talked with him, saying: "As for Me, behold, My covenant is with you, and you shall be a father of many nations. No longer shall your name be called Abram* [Exalted Father]*, but your name shall be Abraham* [Father of a Multitude]*; for I have made you a father of many nations* (Genesis 17:1b-5).

After God changed Abram's name to Abraham, God made an everlasting covenant with him and the Hebrew people.

I will make you exceedingly fruitful; and I will make nations of you, and kings shall come from you. And I will establish My covenant between Me and you and your descendants after you in their generations, for an everlasting covenant, to be God to you and your descendants after you. Also I give to you and your descendants after you the land in which you are a stranger, all the land of Canaan, as an everlasting possession; and I will be their God. (Genesis 17:6-8).

To understand this covenant relationship, it is necessary to recall Abram's ancestry as presented earlier. In addition, it is important to note that Ishmael was born to pre-covenant Abram, and therefore was not included in this new covenant that God made with Abraham and his future covenant son, Isaac. Although Ishmael, along with Abraham and all his male household were called by God to be circumcised as a sign of God's covenant, God rejected Ishmael as the fulfillment of this covenant.

Then God said to Abraham, "As for Sarai your wife, you shall not call her name Sarai, but Sarah [Princess] shall be her name. And I will bless her and also give you a son by her; then I will bless her, and she shall be a mother of nations; kings of peoples shall be from her."

Then Abraham fell on his face and laughed, and said in his heart, "Shall a child be born to a man who is one hundred years old? And shall Sarah, who is ninety years old, bear a child?" And Abraham said to God, "Oh, that Ishmael might live before You!" (Genesis 17:15-18).

While Abraham appeared to have a "How can this be?" moment of honest doubt, apparently he trusted God enough to use him to bring about the promised son of Isaac. How did God respond to Abraham's request that God would be the God of Ishmael as well? He denied Abraham's request.

Then God said: "No, Sarah your wife shall bear you a son, and you shall call his name Isaac; I will establish My covenant with him for an everlasting covenant, and with his descendants after him. And as for Ishmael, I have heard you. Behold, I have blessed him, and will make him fruitful, and will multiply him exceedingly. He shall beget twelve princes, and I will make him a great nation. But My covenant I will establish with Isaac, whom Sarah shall bear to you at this set time next year" (Genesis 17:19-21).

In the verse above, note that this time it was God that told Abraham and Sarah that their son was to be named Isaac. God could not and would not make a covenant with Ishmael, who was born of a slave woman, born of the flesh out of Abram's disobedience and unbelief. God's everlasting covenant had to be made with the free man of Abraham and the son whom God had preordained to be the heir of the free man and whose lineage would give rise to the Jewish Messiah, God's one and only Son, Jesus Christ.

In the beginning of chapter 21 of Genesis, Isaac (Hebrew for "laughter") is born and Abraham circumcises him eight days after his birth. Sarah insisted that Abraham banish Hagar and Ishmael (now 14) from their midst, proclaiming: "Cast out this bondwoman and her son; for the son of this bondwoman shall not be heir with my son, namely with Isaac" (Genesis 21:10). Abraham was distraught, but God said, "Yet I will also make a nation of the son of the bondwoman, because he is your seed [descendant]" (Genesis 21:13). Genesis 21:14 records that Hagar and Ishmael wandered about in the wilderness of Beersheba, an area of the Negev Desert of southern Israel. Ishmael grew up, married an Egyptian woman and lived in the wilderness of Paran, a region of east central Sinai (Genesis 21:20-21), not in Arabia.

Hagar and Ishmael represented the old covenant of the flesh, whereas Abraham, Sarah and Isaac were God's new covenant of the everlasting promise. As important as these foregoing details of

Ishmael's life and his essentiality to the Islamic narrative of faith, such facts are absent from the Qur'an.

Apostle Paul confirmed this reality in his message to the Christians in Galatia. "Now to Abraham and his Seed were the promises made. He does not say, 'And to seeds,' as of many, but as of one, 'And to your Seed,' who is Christ" (Galatians 3:16).

God did not acknowledge Ishmael as Abraham's son. In the Qur'an, there are twelve verses that refer to Allah's covenant with the Jews, but none about Allah having a covenant with Muslims. For example, surah 5:12 states, *And certainly Allah made a covenant with the children of Israel . . .* Other verses affirming Allah's covenant with the Jews are: surah 2:40, 83-84, 93; 3:187; 4:154-155; 5:13, 70; 7:169; 20:80.

In Genesis 22, three times God told Abraham that Isaac was his only son. When God called Abraham to test his faith by sacrificing Isaac, God said: "Take now your son, your only son Isaac, whom you love, and go to the land of Moriah, and offer him there as a burnt offering on one of the mountains of which I shall tell you" (Genesis 22:2).

When Abraham demonstrated that he was willing to obey God and trust Him by sacrificing his only son and the heir of God's covenant with Abraham, God intervened before Abraham drew the blood of Isaac. As Abraham raised the knife, God called out: "Do not lay your hand on the lad, or do anything to him; for now I know that you fear God, since you have not withheld your son, your only son, from Me" (Genesis 22:12).

Then the Angel of the LORD called to Abraham a second time out of heaven, and said: "By Myself I have sworn, says the LORD, because you have done this thing, and have not withheld your son, your only son—blessing I will bless you, and multiplying I will multiply your descendants as the stars of the heaven and as the sand which is on the seashore; and your descendants shall possess the gate of their enemies. In your seed all the nations of the earth shall be blessed, because you have obeyed My voice" (Genesis 22:15-18).

In the Book of Acts, Apostle Paul made it clear that God's covenant with Abraham was fulfilled in Jesus Christ (see Acts 13:32-33, 38- 39). In the lengthy letter to the Hebrews, the writer went into detail on how Jesus was the fulfillment of the old covenant with the institution of a better, new covenant. "But now He [Jesus] has obtained a more excellent ministry, inasmuch as He is also Mediator of a better covenant, which was established on better promises" (Hebrews 8:6).

"By faith Abraham, when he was tested, offered up Isaac, and he who had received the promises offered up his only begotten son," (Hebrews 11:17).

There is no better covenant than that which Jesus inaugurated through His death and resurrection—a covenant of God's mercy, forgiveness and absolving of sins. Muslims have no such covenant and Allah made no such covenant with those who decide to follow him. Therefore, clearly, Islam is not an Abrahamic faith as Muslims have claimed for centuries.

Conclusion. To Abram, God promised to make him the patriarch of a great nation of people and through whom all the nations of the world would be blessed. As for Ishmael, although God did not recognize him as the covenant son that He had promised Abraham, God told Abraham that He would bless Ishmael and make him fruitful and the head of 12 princes (the Ishmaelites) who would disappear long before the birth of Islam.

God also told Hagar, Ishmael's mother, that he would be like a wild donkey and he would be against everyone, and everyone would be against him.

17

Through Abraham and God's promised child of Isaac, God's covenant of a lasting blessing to the nations of the world and the fulfillment of the Messianic prophecy of Jesus Christ would be and was satisfied.

To be clear, according to the Bible, there was and is only one legitimate descendant of Abraham and that was Isaac and the Jewish people. Christians, upon faith in Christ and His sacrificial death on the cross, are adopted into God's Jewish family (see John 1:12-13; Romans 8:15-16; Galatians 4:4-7; Ephesians 1:4-7).

From the present day and historical perspective of the daily violence against mankind by the followers of Islam, it is hard to see that this was God's plan for blessing the nations of the earth through the descendants of Ishmael. Among the descendants of Isaac, however, was Jesus, the sacrificial lamb who brought salvation to the world by the shedding of His blood and not that of another human being—truly a blessing to all who will receive Him.

Endnotes

[i] *Ishmaelites*. Wikipedia. Accessed November 3, 2025.

[ii] *Ismail in Quran*. *The word Ishmael mentioned in the Quran: detail in English and Arabic*. TheLastDialogue, February 8, 2019, Last Updates: October 28, 2025.

[iii] *Did you know? : The Evolution of the Arabic Language in the Silk Roads*. UNESCO.

[iv] *What is the history of the Arabic language?* Alif Arabic, May 8, 2025.

[v] Despite Muslims claiming they are monotheistic, throughout the Qur'an, when Allah speaks it is in the plural "We", "Us", "Our".

[vi] Harb, Ali. *Are Chaldeans Arab?* The Arab American News, February 19, 2016.

[vii] Eph'al, I., 1976. *"Ishmael" and the Arab(s)": A transformation of ethnological terms*. Journal of Near Eastern Studies, 35(4): 225-235.

[viii] Durie, Mark. March 6, 2019. *Ishmael is Not the Father of the Arabs*. Middle East Forum.

[ix] *The Abrahamic Covenant: God's Promise to Abraham*. Fellowship of Israel Related Ministries.

A Special Note to the Seeking Muslim. If you are hungry for God—the One and Only true God of all creation—please read on.

First thing you should know is, that you are not alone. Millions of Muslims around the world, hungry for knowledge of the God of the universe and all creation, have found forgiveness from their sins and peace through a personal, loving relationship with Jesus Christ as God embodied in human flesh for the purpose of a sacrifice for your sin and separation from God.

If you find it hard to accept Christ as God's Son or that God would sacrifice Himself for your sake, you are not alone. However, billions of people over the centuries have trusted and continue to trust and believe that the One and only loving God of Jews and

Christians did exactly that—and it is the only way to salvation and eternal life. No amount of "good works" will bring us into God's presence, in this life or the hereafter.

"For if when we were enemies we were reconciled to God through the death of His Son, much more, having been reconciled, we shall be saved by His life" (Romans 5:10).

Jesus proclaimed, "I am the way, the truth, and the life. No one comes to the Father [God], except through me" (John 14:6).

Pray that God, in the person of Jesus Christ, will reveal Himself to you. Seek Him daily in earnest.

Talk to a Christian friend or co-worker, or seek out a Christian pastor, evangelist or missionary.

Go online if you are able and search for former Muslims who are sharing their testimonies and the Good News of faith in Christ.

Reza Safa, Shahram Hadian, Nabeel Qureshi, Mosab Hassan Yousef, are some who have made the life changing move to salvation in Christ.

If you are unfamiliar with the Bible, borrow one from a Christian or the library, or buy one.

The Sinner's Path to Salvation
BOTTOM LINE!
THIS IS WHERE IT IS AT!

Jesus answered, "I am the way and the truth and the life.
No one comes to the Father except through me.
John 14:6

NOBODY ELSE; NO OTHER DIETY CAN HELP YOU.
*For there is one God and one mediator between
God and mankind, the man Christ Jesus.*
1 Timothy 2:5

*For it is by grace you have been saved,
through faith— and this is not from
yourselves, it is the gift of God—not by works,
so that no one can boast* (Ephesians 2:8-9).

WHAT YOU MUST DO:

1. ADMIT you are a sinner, and that only the Lord
Jesus can save you. Know that no sin is too great
that God cannot forgive. Even if you are or were a
jihadi murderer, God can and will forgive through
your faith in Christ's sacrifice on the cross for you.

*. . . for all have sinned and fall short of the
glory of God* (Romans 3:23).

*He who sins is of the devil, for the devil has
sinned from the beginning. For this purpose the
Son of God was manifested, that He might
destroy the works of the devil* (1 John 3:8).

21

2. **REPENT:** be willing to turn away from sin and submit to God.

   Jesus said: *I tell you, no! But unless you repent, you too will all perish* (Luke 13:5).

   [The Apostle] *Peter replied, "Repent and be baptized, every one of you, in the name of Jesus Christ for the forgiveness of your sins. And you will receive the gift of the Holy Spirit* (Acts 2:38).

3. **BELIEVE** that the Lord Jesus Christ died on the cross and shed his blood to pay the price for your sins, and that he rose again.

   If you declare with your mouth, "Jesus is Lord," and believe in your heart that God raised him from the dead, you will be saved (Romans 10:9).

   God is faithful, by whom you were called into the fellowship of His Son, Jesus Christ our Lord (1 Corinthians 1:9).

4. **ASK** God to save you.

   . . . for, "Everyone who calls on the name of the Lord will be saved."
   Romans 10:13

   I have been crucified with Christ; it is no longer I who live, but Christ lives in me; and the life which I now live in the flesh I live by faith in the Son of God, who loved me and gave Himself for me (Galatians 2:20).

5. **ASK** Jesus Christ to be the Lord (take control) of your life.

Therefore, I urge you, brothers and sisters, in view of God's mercy, to offer your bodies as a living sacrifice, holy and pleasing to God—this is your true and proper worship. Do not conform to the pattern of this world, but be transformed by the renewing of your mind. Then you will be able to test and approve what God's will is—his good, pleasing and perfect will (Romans 12:1-2).

Whoever confesses that Jesus is the Son of God, God abides in him, and he in God (1 John 4:15).

Who is he who overcomes the world, but he who believes that Jesus is the Son of God? (1 John 5:5).

IF YOU REALLY MADE JESUS YOUR LORD, THEN ACT LIKE IT!

1. **Read your Bible** every day to get to know Christ better. *Jesus answered, "It is written: 'Man shall not live on bread alone, but on every word that comes from the mouth of God"* (Matthew 4:4).

2. **Talk to God in prayer** every day. *Pray without ceasing* (1 Thessalonians 5:17).

3. **Find a church** where the Bible is taught as the complete word of God and is the final authority.

*They devoted themselves to the apostles'
teaching and to fellowship, to the breaking of
bread and to prayer* (Acts 2:42).

4. Obey Christ's command to **be baptized**. See
   Acts 2:38 preceding.

5. **Celebrate the Lord's Supper** (communion)
   often. *For whenever you eat this bread and
   drink this cup, you proclaim the Lord's death
   until he comes*   (1 Corinthians 11:26).

6. **Seek forgiveness** (where possible) of those you
   hurt and make restitution where required. Jesus
   said: *This is my blood of the covenant, which is
   poured out for many for the forgiveness of sins*
   (Matthew 26:28).

7. **Forgive unconditionally** others who have
   hurt you. *But if you do not forgive others their
   sins, your Father will not forgive your sins*
   (Matthew 6:15).

8. **Be charitable.** *Each of you should give what
   you have decided in your heart to give, not
   reluctantly or under compulsion, for God loves
   a cheerful giver* (2 Corinthians 9:7).
9. **Share your new faith** with others, both fellow
   believers and non-believers.

   *Therefore go and make disciples of all nations,
   baptizing them in the name of the Father and of
   the Son and of the Holy Spirit,* (Matthew
   28:19).

24

Welcome to the true family of God and His Son, Jesus Christ. God bless you and your journey with Him.

About the Author.

James F. Gauss has been writing for publication since 1962. Since 1998 he has published over two dozen books, most on Christian apologetics. For over twenty years he has been researching, studying and writing about Islam and its comparisons to Christianity.

Author's Books on Islam.

Embracing the Anti-Christ: The Heresy of Interfaith Dialogue (2022)

Islam and Christianity: A Revealing Contrast (2009)

Islam's Deceptions, Lies & False Gospel (2024)

Israel and the Middle East: Will there ever be peace? (2023)

Understanding Islam in the Light of Christianity (Abridged, 2019)

Understanding Islam in the Light of Christianity (Leader & Teacher, 2023)

Understanding Islam in the Light of Christianity (Student, 2023)

www.ingramcontent.com/pod-product-compliance
Lightning Source LLC
Chambersburg PA
CBHW060605030426
42337CB00019B/3624